THREE
BUCKETS

THREE
BUCKETS

A PRACTICAL FRAMEWORK FOR
FOCUS, GROWTH, AND RESULTS

WALLO267

**NANNY'S HOUSE
PUBLISHING**

Pennsauken, New Jersey

Cover Design: Kamera Krew LLC
Interior Design: Jessica Angerstein
Mananging Company: IV MGMT, LLC

Cataloging-in-Publication Data is on file with the Library of Congress.

Paperback ISBN: 979-8-9945002-3-1
ebook ISBN: 979-8-9945002-4-8

1 2 3 4 5 6 7 8 9 10
First edition, January 2026

This book is dedicated to those who chose

RESPONSIBILITY
OVER EXCUSES.

To the people who stopped blaming circumstances
and started organizing their lives with intention.
May these pages remind you that clarity, discipline,
and accountability are not limits but freedom.

Contents

WHY YOU'RE CARRYING TOO MUCH

Most people don't realize when their life stopped feeling manageable. It didn't happen all at once. There wasn't a single moment where everything collapsed. It happened quietly: responsibilities piled up, expectations grew, pressure became normal. And at some point, being overwhelmed stopped feeling temporary and started feeling like a personality trait.

You wake up already tired. Not physically. Mentally. Your body may be rested, but your mind never is. It's already working before your feet touch the floor, thinking about what needs to be done, what you didn't do, what you should have done differently. What might happen. What someone expects from you. What you're behind on. What you can't forget. What you can't afford to mess up.

Even when nothing is actively wrong, you still feel on edge. Like something is coming. Like you're supposed to be doing something right now.

That feeling becomes your baseline.

Most people assume this means they're bad at managing life. They lack discipline, focus, motivation, or emotional control. So they try to fix themselves. They read more books. Watch more videos. Wake up earlier. Push harder. Stay busy. Stay productive. Stay alert.

And still feel heavy.

This book starts with a different assumption. Nothing is wrong with you.

Your mind isn't weak. It's overloaded.

You're not overwhelmed because you can't handle responsibility. You're overwhelmed because you're handling too much at once without a system to organize it.

Think about how many roles you play, how many people rely on you, how many decisions pass through your hands, how many things you're expected to remember, manage, respond to, plan for, and worry about. Then add the pressure of wanting to do it well. Wanting to be better. Wanting to grow. Wanting to not fall behind.

That's not laziness. That's weight.

2

And weight without structure always feels heavier than it needs to be.

What most people are experiencing is not chaos. It's congestion: too many things fighting for the same mental space, too many thoughts being treated as urgent, too many responsibilities being carried without clear timing, and too much noise being mistaken for obligation.

When everything feels important, nothing gets prioritized. When nothing gets prioritized, the mind never rests.

This is where most advice fails people.

You don't need more motivation. You don't need to think positively. You don't need to calm down or let go of responsibility. You need order.

Order is what allows pressure to exist without panic, ambition without burnout, and clarity in loud seasons.

This book is not about mindset. It's about structure.

Mindset matters, but mindset without structure collapses under pressure. Systems hold when emotions fluctuate, work on hard days, work when you're tired, and work when life doesn't slow down.

Three Buckets is a system.

A simple one. On purpose.

Because complex systems break when life gets real.

The goal of this book is not to eliminate responsibility from your life. Responsibility is part of growth. It's part of leadership. It's part of becoming someone reliable and capable. The goal is to help you stop carrying responsibility incorrectly.

Right now, your mind is likely treating everything as if it belongs in the same category: immediate, important, urgent, heavy.

But not everything deserves your energy right now. Not everything needs action, a response, or a decision today.

Until you learn how to separate those things, your mind will continue to feel crowded. And crowded minds don't make clear decisions.

This book will teach you how to divide what you're carrying into three clear categories. What must be handled now. What matters but can wait. And what is simply noise.

That separation alone changes everything.

Because once things are placed correctly, pressure drops. Focus returns. Energy stabilizes. You stop reacting and start deciding.

You stop confusing discomfort with danger, stop promoting thoughts into emergencies, and stop letting noise run your nervous system.

You begin moving with intention instead of urgency.

4

One of the most dangerous lies people believe is that feeling overwhelmed means they're failing. In reality, overwhelm is often the sign of growth without structure. More responsibility came in, but no system was built to hold it.

So instead of building order, people blame themselves.

This book exists to interrupt that cycle.

You don't need to solve your entire life. You need a way to decide what deserves your attention today. And tomorrow. And what can wait without guilt.

You need a way to protect your focus. A way to stop carrying things that aren't yours. A way to honor what matters without rushing it. A way to release what doesn't require action.

That's what the buckets do.

They don't remove pressure. They organize it.

They don't make life easy. They make life clear.

Clarity doesn't mean less responsibility. It means responsibility handled at the right time, in the right way, with the right energy.

As you move through this book, you may notice something uncomfortable at first. You may realize how much energy you've been giving to things that never required it. How many thoughts have you treated like obligations? How many emotions have you tried to solve instead of feeling?

How many emergencies have you created without meaning to?

That awareness is not meant to shame you. It's meant to free you.

Once you see it, you can change it.

This system is not about perfection. You will misplace things sometimes. Everyone does. The power is in returning to the system, not mastering it once.

Every day, life will ask for your attention. The buckets help you decide how to answer.

This book will walk you through why your mind feels heavy, how urgency became a habit, how stress comes from misplacement, and how to use the Three Buckets system to regain control. You'll learn how to handle what truly matters now, how to build long-term progress without anxiety, and how to stop letting noise steal your peace.

By the end, you won't feel like you have less to do. You'll feel like you finally know what deserves your energy.

This is not a mindset shift.

It is a system.

Use it daily. Let it grow with you. And move forward knowing you are no longer reacting to life.

You are leading it.

Chapter One

WHY YOUR MIND FEELS HEAVY

Feeling overwhelmed is a not weakness. It's an unorganized responsibility.

Most people walk around believing something's wrong with them. They think they're lazy, undisciplined, unfocused, or broken because their minds never feel quiet. They tell themselves they should be able to handle more. They look at others who seem calm and assume they're failing at something fundamental. That belief becomes another weight they carry.

But the truth is simpler and more honest.

Your mind feels heavy because it's carrying too much at once, not because it can't carry weight.

There is a difference between being incapable and being overloaded. Incapable means you lack the ability. Overloaded means you have the ability, but too much is stacked on you at the same time. Most people confuse the two. They judge themselves for collapsing under pressure, without realizing that no system functions well when everything demands attention at once.

Your mind was never designed to hold every responsibility, fear, idea, obligation, and expectation simultaneously. It was designed to prioritize. When prioritization breaks down, pressure builds. When pressure builds without structure, overwhelm appears.

That heaviness you feel isn't chaos. It's congestion.

Think about how traffic works. Cars aren't the problem. Roads aren't the problem. The problem happens when too many cars are forced into the same space without direction. Honking starts, tempers rise, and movement slows. Eventually, everything feels stuck. The solution isn't to remove the cars. It's to organize the flow.

Your mind works the same way.

Responsibilities come from everywhere: family needs, financial obligations, health concerns, relationship dynamics, ambitions, regrets, messages, notifications, opinions, expectations, and memories of the past, as well as worries about the future. None of these are wrong on their own. The problem is they all show up at the same time and demand equal attention.

When everything feels important, your brain treats everything like a threat. That's when you start reacting instead of deciding. You move from clarity into survival mode. Survival mode doesn't prioritize well. It scans for danger. It rushes. It over-corrects. It exhausts you.

Many people reading this know survival mode well. Some learned it growing up. Some learned it through instability, loss, poverty, incarceration, betrayal, or chaos. When your life once depended on staying alert, your brain learned to never relax. Even when life improves, the habit remains.

So now you live in a constant state of readiness. Always alert. Always thinking. Always bracing for something. Even good opportunities can feel heavy because your mind doesn't know how to place them. Everything feels like it needs attention now.

That's not a character flaw. That's conditioning.

The problem begins when unorganized responsibility turns into self-judgment. Instead of asking *how to structure what you are carrying*, you ask *what is wrong with you*. That question alone adds more weight. You start carrying shame on top of responsibility, guilt on top of pressure, and comparison on top of effort.

Now your mind isn't just full. It's crowded with emotion.

This is why rest doesn't always feel restful. You can sit still and still feel busy. You can take a break and still feel behind. The heaviness doesn't come from activity. It comes from unresolved placement. Your brain keeps cycling through the same thoughts because it doesn't know where to put them.

People often try to fix this by doing more. More planning. More motivation. More discipline. More self-talk. But adding effort to a disorganized system only increases fatigue. It doesn't create clarity.

Clarity comes from order.

Order doesn't mean control. It means knowing what matters now, what matters later, and what doesn't require your energy at all. Until those distinctions are made, your mind will keep treating everything like it belongs in the same mental space.

That's why you can be productive and still feel overwhelmed. You can be successful and still feel heavy. You can be disciplined and still feel scattered. Productivity without prioritization still leads to exhaustion.

You do not need to think harder. You need to think more clearly.

This book is not asking you to eliminate responsibility. Responsibility is part of growth. It is part of leadership. It is part of building anything meaningful. What needs to change is how you hold it.

When responsibility lacks structure, it becomes pressure. When pressure has no release, it turns into stress. When stress has no explanation, it turns into self-blame.

This chapter exists to interrupt that cycle.

Nothing's wrong with your mind. It's doing exactly what it was trained to do. The issue is that it's been given too many signals at once without a system to organize them.

You're not weak for feeling overwhelmed. You're overloaded without a filter.

Once you understand that, something important shifts. You stop fighting yourself. You stop trying to push through everything at once. You stop confusing urgency with importance. You begin looking for structure instead of motivation.

That is where relief begins.

Not by escaping responsibility, but by learning how to place it correctly.

The heaviness you feel isn't permanent. It's a signal. A signal that your mind needs order, not punishment. Clarity, not criticism. A system, not more pressure.

For now, hold this truth: being overwhelmed is not a weakness; it's an unorganized responsibility.

And anything that can be organized can be handled.

Chapter Two

EVERYTHING IS NOT AN EMERGENCY

How urgency becomes a habit and steals clarity.

Most people aren't stressed because life is constantly on fire. They're stressed because their minds treat everything as if it were. The problem isn't the number of responsibilities they have. It's the way urgency has taken over their thinking.

Urgency feels productive. It feels responsible. It feels like action. But urgency isn't the same thing as importance. When urgency becomes your default setting, clarity disappears.

An emergency is something that requires immediate attention because there are real consequences if it's ignored. Health issues. Safety issues. Legal matters. Financial deadlines. Certain relationship moments. Emergencies are real. They exist. But they're rare.

What happens to most people is that urgency spreads. It leaks into everything. Emails feel urgent. Texts feel urgent. Opinions feel urgent. Thoughts feel urgent. The brain stops asking what actually needs attention now and starts reacting to whatever is loudest.

Urgency becomes a habit.

Once urgency becomes a habit, everything feels like it needs to be handled immediately. Even things that have no deadline. Even things that have no consequence. Even things that are not real yet.

That habit steals clarity.

When your brain lives in a state of urgency, it loses its ability to prioritize. It doesn't ask what matters most. It asks what's closest, loudest, or most uncomfortable. You start confusing relief with progress. You respond just to quiet the feeling, not to solve the issue.

This is why people answer messages they don't need to answer. This is why they make decisions they're not ready to make. This is why they rush conversations that require patience. This is why they feel busy but still behind.

Urgency creates motion without direction.

Many people learned urgency through experience. When you come from environments where things can go wrong quickly, urgency feels safe. Being alert feels responsible. Slowing down feels dangerous. So even when life is stable, your brain stays in high gear.

You don't question urgency because it once protected you.

But what protected you then may now be harming you.

Urgency narrows vision, shortens patience, and reduces judgment. It makes small problems feel massive and large decisions feel rushed. It convinces you that if you don't act right now, something bad will happen.

Most of the time, that fear is false.

The mind under urgency stops distinguishing between discomfort and danger. Discomfort, silence, waiting, even saying no—all of it feels like an emergency.

So you act.

You respond too quickly. You over explain. You over commit. You overthink. You overreact.

Afterward, you feel tired, regretful, or unclear. And then you blame yourself for not handling it better.

The truth is, urgency robbed you of clarity before you ever made the decision.

Clarity does not live in panic. It lives in space.

You can't ignore responsibility. You have to slow urgency down long enough to ask a better question: *Is this truly urgent, or is it just uncomfortable?*

Urgent means there is a consequence if you don't act now. Uncomfortable means your mind wants relief. Those two things are not the same.

Urgency thrives on emotion. Clarity thrives on structure. Without structure, emotion takes control, and emotion doesn't prioritize well.

Think about how many times you felt pressure to respond immediately, only to realize later nothing would have happened if you waited. Think about how many decisions you rushed because you wanted the feeling to stop. That is urgency doing its job, pushing you toward relief, not resolution.

Urgency loves immediacy. It hates patience, silence, and reflection. But reflection is where good decisions are made. When urgency is constant, your nervous system never rests. Even when nothing is happening, your body feels like something should be. That's why rest can feel uncomfortable, silence can feel loud, and calm can feel suspicious.

So you fill the space.

You scroll, you plan, you worry, you revisit conversations, you rehearse outcomes, you create scenarios. None of these things are emergencies, but urgency convinces you they are.

That constant mental activity becomes exhausting.

You were not meant to live like this.

The goal is not to eliminate urgency entirely. The goal is to contain it. To reserve it for moments that truly require it and to stop letting urgency bleed into every area of your life.

This is where discipline comes in. Not discipline as punishment, but discipline as active decision making.

The discipline to pause before responding,e to sit with discomfort, to let things wait when they can. Waiting is not avoidance.

When you slow urgency down, clarity returns, and you can see things for what they are instead of how they feel. You stop reacting to noise, and you start responding to reality.

This is the shift.

You do not need to live in constant alertness to be responsible. You do not need to rush to be productive. You do not need urgency to prove you care.

Calm decisions are not careless decisions.

Urgency tells you everything matters *now*. Clarity prioritizes.

Once you understand that everything is not an emergency, your mind begins to breathe again.

Chapter Three

STRESS COMES FROM MISPLACEMENT

W hy most pressure is self-created by putting things in the wrong mental category.

Stress rarely comes from what is happening; it comes from how what is happening is being held.

Two people can face the same situation and experience completely different levels of pressure. One can feel grounded. The other can feel overwhelmed. The difference is not strength, intelligence, or resilience. The difference is placement.

When your mind does not know where something belongs, it treats it like it belongs everywhere. That is when pressure multiplies.

Most stress isn't caused by too much responsibility. It's caused by responsibility sitting in the wrong place.

Thoughts meant for later are treated like they must be handled now, feelings meant to be acknowledged are treated like problems that must be solved, and noise is treated like an obligation.

Once that happens, everything starts competing for the same mental space.

Your brain doesn't have unlimited shelves. It has limited attention. When everything is placed on the same shelf, nothing is stable. You keep revisiting the same issues, not because they're unresolved, but because they're misplaced.

This is why your mind circles.

You think about things you can't act on yet, worry about outcomes you can't control, replay conversations that are already over, and stress about future responsibilities that aren't ready for attention.

None of those things are wrong to think about. They're wrong to carry as if they require immediate action.

Misplacement turns thinking into pressure.

A simple example makes this clear. Imagine carrying groceries. If everything is placed into one bag, it becomes heavy and unstable. Items fall, the bag strains, and you struggle. The solution isn't fewer groceries. The solution is distributing the weight correctly.

Your mind works the same way.

When you place future tasks into the present moment, they add weight where it doesn't belong. When you place imagined outcomes into your decision-making, they steal focus. When you take on other people's expectations, they drain your energy.

You start feeling stressed even when nothing is actually happening.

This is where many people misunderstand stress. They assume stress is a sign that they need to do something immediately. In reality, stress is often a signal that something's sitting in the wrong category.

Stress is information.

It tells you something needs to be moved, not necessarily acted on.

Most people respond to stress by pushing harder. They try to solve everything at once, stacking effort on top of confusion. That only increases fatigue.

What they really need is reassignment.

This chapter exists to show you that pressure decreases not when life becomes lighter, but when clarity about placement increases.

Think about how many things you carry that have no action attached to them right now. Thoughts like: *What if this doesn't work? What if I disappoint someone? What if I fall behind? What if something goes wrong later?*

Those thoughts feel heavy because they're being treated like current problems. But they're not current problems. They're future possibilities.

Possibilities do not require immediate action. They require planning or acceptance, not panic.

When you put future possibilities into the present bucket, stress spikes.

The same thing happens with emotions. Emotions are signals. They are meant to be felt, not fixed. When you treat feelings like problems, you start carrying them as responsibilities.

You feel guilt and think you need to do something, feel anxiety and think you need answers, or feel discomfort and think you need relief.

So you act. You over explain. You over-commit. You over-think. Not because it is required, but because the feeling is misplaced.

Emotions don't belong in the same category as obligations. They belong to awareness.

Misplacement also shows up in how people carry other people. Someone else's disappointment becomes your emergency. Someone else's expectations become your deadline. Someone else's opinion becomes your problem.

None of that is true responsibility.

When you carry things that are not yours, stress becomes inevitable.

This is why people who lack boundaries feel constantly pressured. They're not carrying more responsibility. They're carrying misassigned responsibility.

Once you understand this, stress stops feeling mysterious. You can trace it back. You can ask a simple question: *Does this require action now*, or *is it just sitting in the wrong place?*

That question alone reduces pressure.

The goal isn't to eliminate thinking. The goal is to place thinking where it belongs. Reflection has a place. Planning has a place. Action has a place. Rest has a place.

When those things blend together, clarity disappears. Stress thrives in blur. Clarity thrives in separation.

This is why you can feel stressed on a day when nothing actually goes wrong. Your mind is holding things that do not belong to today.

This is also why stress can disappear quickly when something is clearly defined. Once you know what needs to be done now, what can wait, and what does not require action at all, pressure drops.

Not because the situation changed, but because placement did. You do not need to carry everything at once to be responsible. In fact, carrying everything at once is irresponsible to your mind and body. Responsibility means handling things when they are ready to be handled.

Misplacement convinces you that readiness does not matter.

This chapter prepares you for the shift that comes next. Once you understand that stress comes from misplacement, not life itself, you are ready for a system. A way to assign things correctly. A way to stop letting everything live in the same mental space.

That system is coming.

For now, remember this.

If you feel pressure without a clear action, something's likely out of place. Move it, schedule it, release it, or simply acknowledge it without acting.

Stress fades when placement is corrected.

Clarity begins the moment you stop carrying what does not belong in the present.

Chapter Four

THE THREE BUCKETS EXPLAINED

A simple system to separate reality from reaction.

Once you understand that overwhelm comes from unorganized responsibility, that urgency is a habit, and that stress comes from misplacement, the next question becomes obvious: *How do you actually organize what you're carrying?*

Not emotionally. Not philosophically. Practically.

You need a system that works when life is loud. Not when everything is calm. Not when you have time to reflect. But when pressure is present, decisions are required.

That is what the Three Buckets are.

The Three Buckets system exists to answer one question clearly and consistently: *What deserves my energy right now?*

Most people never answer that question. They just react to whatever shows up. The Three Buckets force clarity before action.

This system is simple by design. Simplicity isn't weakness. Simplicity is what holds under pressure. Complex systems collapse when life speeds up. Simple systems endure.

The Three Buckets aren't about removing responsibility. They're about assigning it correctly.

Bucket One is what must be handled now.

Bucket Two is what matters, but can wait.

Bucket Three is what feels heavy but requires no action.

Everything in your life fits into one of these three categories. Everything.

If it does not fit, you are either avoiding honesty or resisting clarity.

Most people struggle because they treat all three buckets the same. They give everything equal urgency. Equal emotional weight. Equal attention. That is where overwhelm is born.

The moment you separate these buckets, something changes. Your mind stops spinning—not because problems disappear, but because they stop competing.

Let's break this down clearly.

Bucket One isn't for things that feel uncomfortable, cause anxiety, or create guilt. It's for things that truly break something if left untouched. When Bucket One is clear, panic disappears. You know exactly what needs attention and move with purpose.

Health issues that can't wait. Legal matters with deadlines. Financial responsibilities with penalties. Safety concerns. Critical relationship moments that require immediate presence.

Bucket One is small, much smaller than most people think. The mistake people make is putting too much into it.

Bucket One isn't for things that feel uncomfortable, cause anxiety, or create guilt. It's for things that truly break something if left untouched. When Bucket One is clear, panic disappears. You know exactly what needs attention. You stop guessing. You stop reacting. You move with purpose.

Bucket Two is where growth lives. This is where long-term progress happens. Planning. Healing. Building. Learning. Improving. Strategizing. Creating.

Bucket Two matters deeply. It does not require urgency. It requires consistency.

This is where most people fail themselves. They either ignore Bucket Two completely or try to rush it like an emergency. Both paths destroy progress.

When you ignore Bucket Two, nothing improves. When you rush Bucket Two, you burn out.

Bucket Two requires patience and scheduling.

Bucket Three is the most misunderstood and most dangerous when mismanaged. Bucket Three is noise.

Noise isn't meaningless. It just doesn't require action.

Thoughts about what people think. Comparisons. Old conversations. Future worries with no current solution. Guilt without instruction. Opinions without authority.

Noise feels heavy because it consumes attention without producing movement.

Most people live in Bucket Three while thinking they are being responsible. They spend mental energy on things they cannot act on. That creates exhaustion without progress.

The Three Buckets system demands honesty. You can't place things based on how they feel. You place them based on consequence and timing.

This is where discipline enters.

Discipline is not forcing yourself to do more. Discipline is refusing to lie to yourself about what matters right now.

The buckets don't change based on mood. They change based on reality.

When you sit down to organize your life using this system, something uncomfortable happens at first. You realize how much energy you have been giving to noise. How many things did you treat like emergencies that were never urgent? How many real priorities were ignored because they were not loud?

That realization isn't meant to shame you. It's meant to free you.

Once something is placed correctly, it stops haunting you. Bucket One gets handled. Bucket Two gets scheduled. Bucket Three gets acknowledged and released.

This is why the system works.

You're not suppressing thoughts. You're assigning them.

Assignment brings relief.

Most mental stress comes from trying to remember everything. The buckets remove that burden. You no longer have to hold everything in your head. You just have to know where it belongs.

This is not about perfection. It is about clarity.

Some days Bucket One will be full. Some days it will be light. Some days Bucket Two will demand more time. Some days Bucket Three will be loud. The system adapts. You do not.

You return to the same question every time: *What bucket does this belong in?*

That question alone interrupts panic.

The Three Buckets are about order. And order is what the mind needs to feel safe.

When the mind knows that urgent things are being handled, important things are being honored, and noise is not in charge, it relaxes. Focus returns. Energy stabilizes.

This isn't a mindset shift. It's a structural shift.

You stop asking, *How do I feel?* and start asking, *What is required?*

You stop reacting and start deciding.

This chapter is the foundation. Everything that follows builds on this structure. The next chapters will teach you how to use each bucket correctly and how to protect them from collapsing into each other.

For now, understand this.

Clarity is not about having fewer problems.

It is about knowing where each problem belongs.

Once placement is correct, pressure drops and movement becomes possible.

Chapter Five

BUCKET ONE: WHAT MUST BE HANDLED NOW

How to identify real consequences and act without panic

Bucket One is the smallest bucket, but it carries the most weight, not because it holds more items but because the items inside it have consequences.

Bucket One isn't about what feels urgent. It is about what is urgent.

This distinction matters because most people overload Bucket One with emotion instead of reality. They confuse pressure with consequence. They confuse anxiety with obligation. The result is constant panic, even when very little actually needs immediate action.

Bucket One exists to protect you from that.

Something belongs in Bucket One only if ignoring it creates real damage in the near term. Damage that is tangible. Measurable. Undeniable.

Health situations that can't wait. Legal deadlines with penalties. Financial obligations with immediate consequences. Safety issues. Moments where presence is required to prevent harm or loss.

That is it.

Bucket One doesn't include discomfort, embarrassment, fear of disappointing someone, imagined outcomes, or urgency created by someone else's anxiety.

If the consequence is only emotional discomfort, it does not belong in Bucket One.

This is where many people struggle. Discomfort feels threatening, especially if you have lived in survival mode. Your nervous system reacts to discomfort as if it were danger. So you rush to fix it.

Bucket One teaches you to slow down that reaction.

Before placing anything into Bucket One, ask one question: *If I don't handle this in the next seventy-two hours, what actually breaks?*

If the answer is nothing tangible, it doesn't belong there.

That question alone will dramatically reduce your stress.

Bucket One is meant to be clear and contained. When it is clear, panic fades. When it is contained, focus sharpens.

The danger comes when Bucket One becomes a dumping ground. Every thought, request, message, and emotion gets thrown into it. Once that happens, you lose the ability to see what truly matters.

You start treating everything like a fire. And when everything is a fire, you burn out.

Bucket One requires honesty and restraint.

There is also something important to understand about Bucket One. Acting quickly does not mean acting frantically. Speed without clarity creates mistakes. Bucket One is about decisive action, not rushed action.

When something truly belongs in Bucket One, the path forward is usually clear. There's a phone call to make, a payment to handle, an appointment to attend, a conversation that can't wait.

These actions are specific. They are not vague. If you can't identify a clear action, the issue may not belong in Bucket One.

Clarity is a signal of correct placement.

Another common mistake is carrying Bucket One items mentally instead of acting on them. People replay urgent situations in their head over and over instead of addressing them. That doesn't create safety. It creates exhaustion.

Bucket One is meant for execution, not rumination.

Once you identify something as truly urgent, act. Handle it. Close the loop. Do not let it live in your mind longer than necessary.

Handling Bucket One items restores trust in yourself. Your mind relaxes when it knows you will act when action is required. That trust reduces anxiety across all areas of life.

There is also a boundary lesson here. Not everything someone labels as urgent is urgent for you. Other people will try to place their priorities into your Bucket One. They will use tone, pressure, guilt, or volume to do it.

Your job is to protect the bucket.

Ask the same question: *What actually breaks if this waits?*

If the answer is nothing on your side, it doesn't belong in your Bucket One.

This isn't selfishness. It's responsibility.

When Bucket One is protected, you stop living reactively. You stop letting other people's urgency dictate your nervous system.

This is especially important for leaders, parents, entrepreneurs, and caretakers. The more capable you are, the more people will try to hand their emergencies to you.

You must decide which ones are real.

There's peace in knowing that when something truly matters, you'll show up. And when it doesn't, you won't allow panic to steal your energy.

Bucket One is about respect. Respect for reality. Respect for timing. Respect for your mental health.

When you stop flooding Bucket One, something powerful happens. You regain confidence in your ability to handle life. You stop feeling behind. You stop waking up already stressed.

You realize how few things actually require immediate attention.

That realization is freeing.

Bucket One does not run your life. It protects it.

When you learn to identify what truly must be handled now and act without panic, you reclaim control over your time, your focus, and your peace.

Chapter Six

STOP CREATING
FAKE EMERGENCIES

Noise keeps getting promoted to priority.

Most of the pressure people live under isn't coming from real emergencies. It is coming from fake ones they unknowingly create and then respond to as if something is at stake.

Fake emergencies are convincing because they feel urgent. They trigger emotion and demand attention. But they have one thing in common: nothing actually breaks if they're ignored.

The problem is that your nervous system doesn't know the difference unless you teach it.

Fake emergencies are born when noise gets mistaken for responsibility.

A thought pops up. A message comes in. A feeling shows up. An opinion is expressed.

And immediately your body reacts. Heart rate changes. Focus shifts. You feel pressure to respond, fix, explain, decide, or act.

That reaction happens before logic ever enters the conversation.

Most people never pause long enough to ask whether the urgency is real. They just move. And over time, this becomes a habit: noise gets upgraded to priority, discomfort gets upgraded to danger, and thoughts get upgraded to tasks.

This is how fake emergencies take over your life.

A fake emergency feels like something bad will happen if you don't act immediately. But when you slow it down and examine it honestly, there's no actual consequence tied to timing. The urgency is emotional, not factual.

Someone is upset. Someone expects a response. Someone misunderstands you. Someone disagrees with you. You feel behind. You feel uncertain.

None of those are emergencies by default.

They feel urgent because emotion is loud. Emotion wants resolution, relief, and certainty. But urgency driven by emotion doesn't lead to clarity. It leads to a reaction.

Reaction creates more noise.

This is why people feel like they are constantly putting out fires. They are not fires. They are sparks. And sparks only become fires when you feed them attention.

One of the most powerful shifts you can make is learning to sit with discomfort without turning it into action. Discomfort isn't an instruction. It's a sensation.

Fake emergencies rely on one lie: that acting now will make the feeling go away.

Sometimes it does. Temporarily. But it often creates bigger problems later. You say yes when you should have waited. You respond when silence would have served you. You make a decision without enough information. You overcommit. You overexplain. You give energy where none was required.

Then you feel drained.

The mind interprets that drain as a greater sense of urgency. So the cycle repeats.

Fake emergencies multiply because they are never questioned.

This chapter is about questioning them.

Anytime you feel pressure, stop and ask a simple question: *What happens if I do nothing for twenty-four hours?*

If the answer is nothing tangible, you're likely dealing with a fake emergency.

That pause is powerful. It interrupts the automatic response. It gives clarity and space to enter.

Fake emergencies often come from three sources.

The first is other people's urgency. Someone *else* is anxious. Someone else wants a quick answer. Someone else is uncomfortable waiting. They hand that feeling to you. If you accept it, it becomes your emergency.

You are not required to carry other people's urgency.

The second source is internal discomfort. Anxiety hates uncertainty. It wants closure. So it creates urgency where none exists. Your job is to recognize when your body is reacting to discomfort, not danger.

The third source is imagined outcomes. Your mind runs ahead. It predicts problems. It creates scenarios. Then it reacts to those scenarios as if they are happening now.

Imagined futures don't belong in present action.

When fake emergencies run your life, everything feels exhausting. You're constantly responding but rarely progressing, busy but not moving forward.

This is why people feel behind even when they are active.

Real progress requires focus. Focus requires boundaries. Boundaries require discernment.

Stopping fake emergencies is not about becoming cold or detached. It is about becoming accurate.

Accuracy means responding to what is real, not what is loud.

When you stop prioritizing noise, your energy returns. Your focus sharpens. Your decisions improve.

You begin to notice how few things truly require immediate action.

This does not mean you ignore people or responsibilities. It means you respond on your terms, not your nervous system's.

You start answering messages when you have clarity, not pressure. You start making decisions when you have information, not anxiety. You start protecting your time instead of reacting to demands.

Fake emergencies lose their power when they are named.

The moment you say, *This does not require action right now*, something shifts inside you. Your body relaxes. Your mind slows. You regain choice.

Choice is the opposite of urgency.

Once you stop creating fake emergencies, you free up energy. That energy needs direction. That direction lives in the long game.

Now you need to learn how to handle what matters deeply without rushing it and how Bucket Two becomes the foundation for sustainable progress.

Chapter Seven

BUCKET TWO: THE LONG GAME

How rushing growth destroys progress.

Bucket Two is where most people say they care and then live like they don't.

Not because they're dishonest, but because Bucket Two doesn't scream. It doesn't panic. It doesn't demand attention the way emergencies do. It waits quietly and patiently. And because it waits, it often gets ignored or mishandled.

Bucket Two is where your future lives.

This bucket holds the things that matter deeply but don't require immediate action: growth, healing, planning, building, learning, creating, improving relationships, strengthening health, developing skills, and designing the life you want instead of just managing the one you have.

Bucket Two is not urgent, but it is essential.

Most people struggle with Bucket Two in one of two ways. They either neglect it completely or treat it like an emergency. Both are destructive.

Neglect looks like constantly saying you'll get to it later. Later never comes because Bucket One and fake emergencies keep taking priority. Years pass. Nothing changes. Frustration builds. People begin to feel stuck, even though they are busy.

Rushing looks like trying to force progress on a timeline driven by anxiety instead of reality. People want results now, healing now, success now, clarity now. So they push, overwork, and expect quick transformation. When it doesn't happen fast enough, they quit or judge themselves.

Both paths lead to the same place: burnout and disappointment.

Bucket Two requires a different approach.

Bucket Two needs consistency, not urgency.

Urgency is useful in Bucket One. In Bucket Two, urgency poisons progress. Growth does not respond well to pressure. It responds to repetition, patience, and trust.

Think about anything meaningful you've built: strength, skill, relationships, confidence. None of it happened in a rush. It happened slowly, often quietly, through repeated effort that didn't always feel dramatic.

Bucket Two is uncomfortable because it demands faith: faith that small actions add up, faith that progress is happening even when you can't see it yet, and faith that you don't need to force outcomes to deserve them.

This is hard for people who come from a survival mode. Survival teaches you to move fast or lose. Bucket Two teaches you to move steadily or break.

That shift feels unnatural at first.

Many people sabotage Bucket Two because they feel guilty giving it time. They think if something matters, it should be urgent, and if it's not urgent, it must be optional.

That belief is wrong.

Bucket Two is what prevents Bucket One from controlling your life forever.

When you neglect Bucket Two, emergencies multiply. Health issues appear, financial pressure grows, relationships strain, and opportunities are missed. Suddenly, everything feels urgent again.

Bucket Two is preventative.

It is how you reduce future pressure.

This is why the most disciplined people schedule Bucket Two intentionally. They don't wait for motivation. They don't wait for free time. They make space for it because they understand its role.

Bucket Two does not need your anxiety. It needs your commitment.

Another mistake people make is expecting Bucket Two to feel rewarding right away. It often doesn't. Early progress is invisible, and early effort feels small. That's why many people quit too soon.

They confuse slow growth with no growth.

Consistency beats urgency every time.

Doing a little every day builds momentum, momentum builds confidence, and confidence sustains action. This is the cycle Bucket Two relies on.

Bucket Two also requires forgiveness: forgiveness for missed days, missed weeks, and missed seasons. Shame kills consistency. Grace restores it.

You don't need to catch up. You need to start where you are.

Bucket Two isn't about intensity. It's about reliability.

One of the most powerful things you can do is decide when Bucket Two gets your energy. Schedule it. Protect it. Treat it with respect.

That could mean dedicated time, dedicated space, and dedicated boundaries. It doesn't have to be dramatic. It just has to be consistent.

When Bucket Two is honored, something subtle happens. Life feels less frantic. Even when Bucket One gets busy, you don't feel lost because you know progress is happening somewhere deeper.

This reduces anxiety.

People often feel anxious because they don't trust their future. Bucket Two builds that trust.

You begin to believe that, even if today is chaotic, tomorrow is being handled. That belief creates calm.

Bucket Two also teaches patience. Not passive patience, but active patience. The kind that shows up consistently without demanding immediate reward.

This is maturity.

You stop measuring progress by speed and start measuring it by alignment.

You stop rushing growth and start allowing it to unfold.

When Bucket Two is handled correctly, pressure decreases across all areas of life. Emergencies feel less frequent. Decisions feel less reactive. Confidence grows quietly.

Without Bucket Two, the system collapses into survival. With it, life becomes intentional.

The next thing to learn is how to work Bucket Two without anxiety and how consistency becomes your greatest advantage.

Chapter Eight

CONSISTENCY BEATS URGENCY

Building momentum without anxiety.

Urgency promises quick results. Consistency delivers lasting ones.

Most people know this intellectually, but they don't live it. They chase bursts of effort instead of building rhythms, sprint when patience is required, and mistake intensity for commitment. And when the rush fades, they assume something's wrong.

Nothing is wrong. Urgency simply wore off.

Urgency is loud. It feels powerful. It makes you feel productive. But urgency is fueled by emotion. When emotion changes, urgency disappears. Consistency does not depend on emotion. It depends on structure.

That is why consistency wins.

This chapter exists to help you understand how to build momentum without anxiety, because anxiety makes urgency feel necessary. It convinces you that if you don't move fast, you'll miss your chance, fall behind, or fail.

But anxiety lies.

Progress doesn't respond to panic. It responds to repetition.

Most people abandon consistency because it feels boring. There's no adrenaline, no immediate payoff, no dramatic before and after. But boring is often where transformation lives.

The mind raised on urgency struggles with steadiness. It wants results now, feedback now, relief now. So it keeps switching strategies, starting and stopping, committing and quitting.

Consistency requires you to tolerate the quiet.

Quiet effort feels invisible. It doesn't get applause or feel impressive. But it compounds.

Compounding is the real power.

One small action repeated daily does more than one big action done once. This applies to everything: health, finances, skills, relationships, and mental clarity.

Consistency creates trust: trust in yourself, trust in the process, and trust that progress is happening even when you don't feel it.

Urgency erodes trust. You rush, make emotional decisions, burn energy, then stop. That pattern trains your brain not to trust your own follow-through.

This is why many people feel stuck. They don't trust themselves to stick with anything, not because they're incapable, but because urgency taught them to move in bursts instead of patterns.

Consistency repairs that trust.

The key to consistency is lowering the threshold. Most people aim too high and quit. They demand too much from themselves and call it discipline. It's not discipline—it's pressure.

Real discipline is sustainable.

If you need motivation to do it, it's probably too big.

Consistency works when the action is small enough to repeat even on bad days.

That might mean ten minutes instead of an hour, one page instead of a chapter, one conversation instead of a full plan, or one task completed instead of a full reset.

Small wins create momentum. Momentum reduces anxiety.

Anxiety thrives when things feel unfinished, while completion, even in small doses, calms the mind. This is why one completed task can change your entire day.

Consistency also requires boundaries. You must protect the time and energy you've assigned to Bucket Two. Urgency will try to steal it, fake emergencies will try to interrupt it, and other people's demands will try to override it.

You must decide in advance that Bucket Two matters even when it doesn't feel urgent.

This is how long-term change is built.

Consistency doesn't mean rigidity. It means reliability. If you miss a day, you return the next. If you fall off, you get back on—without drama, without self-punishment.

Anxiety tells you that missed time equals failure. Consistency says missed time equals adjustment.

This mindset shift is subtle but powerful.

Consistency also teaches patience with yourself. You stop expecting instant transformation, stop rushing growth, and allow yourself to become.

Becoming takes time.

Urgency wants the finish line. Consistency focuses on the next step.

When you focus on the next step, the path reveals itself.

This chapter matters because it gives you a way to move forward without burning out. It shows you how to make progress feel manageable instead of overwhelming.

When consistency becomes your default, urgency loses its grip. You no longer feel the need to rush. You trust your system, your schedule, and yourself.

This creates calm. Calm creates clarity. Clarity allows better decisions.

This is how momentum is built without anxiety.

The next bucket steals the most energy when ignored or misunderstood.

Chapter Nine

BUCKET THREE
THE NOISE

Guilt, comparison, opinions, and thoughts that drain energy.

Bucket Three holds the most weight and the least responsibility.

This is the bucket that exhausts people without ever producing progress. The bucket that keeps minds busy and bodies tired. The bucket most people live in while thinking they are being productive.

Bucket Three is noise.

Noise is anything that consumes your attention without requiring action. It feels heavy because it occupies space, not because it demands responsibility. The danger of noise is not that it exists. The danger is that it feels important.

Noise comes in many forms.

Guilt that has no instruction. Comparison that has no direction. Opinions that have no authority. Thoughts about what people think. Replaying old conversations. Imagining future outcomes you can't control.

None of these things requires action right now. But they demand attention. And attention is energy.

When attention is drained without movement, exhaustion follows.

Most people never identify noise for what it is. They treat it like an obligation, feel responsible for resolving feelings that were never meant to be solved, try to answer questions that don't have answers, and attempt to satisfy expectations that were never clearly stated.

That's why Bucket Three is so dangerous.

Noise is convincing because it feels personal. It attaches to identity. It whispers things like, *you should be doing more, you should be further along, you should respond, you should fix this*, and *you should explain yourself.*

But "should" is not an instruction. It is a pressure word.

Bucket Three thrives on "shoulds."

The mind doesn't know how to rest when noise is untreated. Even in quiet moments, noise shows up. You try to relax and suddenly remember something embarrassing, lie down to sleep, and your mind starts replaying conversations, or feel good for a moment, and then comparison steals it.

This isn't because something needs to be done. It's because noise wants attention.

One of the biggest mistakes people make is trying to eliminate noise. You cannot. Noise is part of being human. The goal is not elimination. The goal is containment.

Noise belongs in Bucket Three, so it stops running the other buckets.

When noise goes unnamed, it sneaks into Bucket One and creates fake emergencies. It sneaks into Bucket Two and creates anxiety. It tells you to rush, compare, judge, and doubt.

Once noise is identified, it loses power.

A thought doesn't become true because it's loud. A feeling doesn't become urgent because it's uncomfortable.

Noise becomes dangerous when it is believed without examination.

This chapter teaches you to stop arguing with noise and start recognizing it.

You do not need to debate every thought. You need to categorize it.

If a thought has no action attached to it right now, it belongs in Bucket Three. If a feeling has no instruction, it belongs in Bucket Three. If an opinion doesn't come from someone whose life you want, it belongs in Bucket Three.

This is not avoidance. This is discernment.

Bucket Three is also where social pressure lives: expectations that were never agreed to, standards that were never chosen, and timelines that were never yours.

Comparison is one of the loudest forms of noise. It convinces you that someone else's path is your measuring stick, that their speed should be your speed, and that their outcome invalidates your progress.

Comparison steals peace without offering direction.

Guilt is another heavy form of noise. Especially guilt that has no clear cause or solution. Guilt that exists simply because you feel like you should be doing more.

That guilt does not require action. It requires awareness and release.

Opinions also live in Bucket Three. Everyone has them, but few are relevant, many are uninformed, and some are projections.

You do not owe every opinion your energy.

One of the most freeing realizations in life is understanding that not everything that enters your mind deserves to stay there.

Bucket Three gives you permission to release without resolving.

This is where many people struggle. They think letting go means ignoring. It doesn't—it means acknowledging without engaging.

You can notice a thought without following it, feel a feeling without acting on it, and hear an opinion without internalizing it.

That is strength.

When Bucket Three is managed properly, mental space opens up, focus improves, emotional reactivity decreases, and you stop feeling pulled in ten directions.

This also improves relationships. You stop responding defensively, stop explaining unnecessarily, and stop carrying other people's emotions as your responsibility.

You become steadier.

Noise will still show up. That is normal. The difference is it no longer runs your system.

You recognize it, place it, and move on.

This chapter matters because most people believe their exhaustion comes from life. In reality, it comes from how much noise they are entertaining.

When you stop giving noise authority, energy returns.

Bucket Three doesn't require fixing. It requires boundaries.

Next, you need to know how to protect those boundaries and keep your focus intact so the system does not collapse under pressure.

Chapter Ten

PROTECT YOUR FOCUS

Boundaries, discipline, and learning to say no without guilt.

Focus is not about concentration. It is about protection.

Most people think they struggle with focus because they lack discipline or willpower. In reality, they struggle with focus because they haven't built boundaries around their attention. They allow too many things to access their mind, their time, and their emotional energy.

Focus disappears when everything has permission.

The Three Buckets system only works if the buckets are protected. Without boundaries, noise spills into urgency. Other people's priorities override your own. Fake emergencies steal time meant for growth. Eventually, everything collapses back into chaos.

This chapter is about protecting the system.

Boundaries are not walls. They are filters. They decide what gets through and what does not. Without them, your focus will always be at the mercy of whoever is loudest, closest, or most demanding.

Many people avoid boundaries because they associate them with conflict. They worry about disappointing others, being misunderstood, or being seen as selfish. So they say yes when they should pause, respond when they should wait, and explain when silence would serve them better.

That behavior erodes focus.

Saying yes to everything isn't kindness. It's surrender.

Every yes costs you something: time, energy, and attention. When you say yes without intention, you spend resources you can't get back.

Protecting focus means being intentional with your yes and your no.

A no does not require justification. It requires clarity.

Guilt often shows up when people first start setting boundaries. That guilt isn't a sign you're doing something wrong. It's a sign you're breaking an old pattern, especially if you've been conditioned to be available, helpful, or agreeable to feel worthy.

Guilt fades when boundaries become normal.

Discipline plays a role here—not discipline as punishment, but discipline as commitment: commitment to your priorities, commitment to your energy, and commitment to honoring what you've placed in each bucket.

Discipline means you don't renegotiate with urgency, don't let emotion override structure, and return to the system even when it feels uncomfortable.

Protecting focus also means protecting time. Time is where buckets are honored: Bucket One gets handled, Bucket Two gets scheduled, and Bucket Three gets limited access.

If everything is allowed to interrupt you, nothing gets completed.

Completion is what calms the mind.

This is why one of the most powerful boundaries you can set is around responsiveness. You don't need to be instantly available to be responsible or respond immediately to prove you care.

Response time is not a measure of character.

When you control when you respond, you control your nervous system.

Another aspect of focus protection is the environment. Your surroundings either support clarity or sabotage it.

Noise isn't just mental. It's physical: notifications, conversations, and media all compete for attention.

Protecting focus means choosing environments that align with your priorities when possible.

This chapter is also about learning to disappoint people without abandoning yourself. Someone will always want more than you can give. If you try to satisfy every expectation, you will exhaust yourself.

You are allowed to choose where your energy goes.

Protecting focus is not selfish. It is responsible.

When your focus is protected, the buckets stay intact. You stop feeling pulled, stop feeling scattered, and stop feeling like you're constantly reacting.

You move with intention.

Boundaries also create respect. When people know your limits, they treat your time differently. When you respect your own focus, others often follow.

But even if they don't, your responsibility is to yourself.

Without focus, even the best system fails. Focus is the gatekeeper. It ensures that what matters gets attention and what does not is filtered out.

When you protect your focus, clarity becomes sustainable. You are no longer constantly starting over. You are building.

Even one small completed action can restore control and calm when everything feels heavy.

Chapter Eleven

ONE WIN CHANGES EVERYTHING

Why completing one task restores control and calm.

When people feel overwhelmed, they usually think they need a breakthrough. Something big. Something dramatic. A full reset. A complete plan. A perfect day to start over.

That belief keeps them stuck.

What they actually need is one win.

Overwhelm thrives on incompletion. The mind feels heavy when nothing feels finished. Open loops stack up, tasks linger, and decisions remain half-made. The brain keeps everything active because nothing has been closed.

That constant openness creates pressure.

Completion does the opposite. It tells the brain something is handled. That signal creates relief, not because the entire problem is solved, but because progress has been made.

One completed task can quiet dozens of unfinished thoughts.

This is why small wins matter more than big intentions.

Most people underestimate the psychological impact of completion. They chase motivation instead of closure and wait to feel ready instead of finishing something small.

But readiness is unreliable. Completion is grounding.

When you finish one thing, your nervous system relaxes, your focus sharpens, your confidence stabilizes, and you feel capable again.

That feeling changes how you approach everything else.

This chapter teaches you how to use one win as a tool.

One win doesn't mean the most important task. It means the most clear task, the one with a visible finish line, the one you can complete without debate.

Send the email. Make the call. Pay the bill. Schedule the appointment. Write the paragraph.

These actions may feel small, but they create momentum.

Momentum is not speed. It is a direction.

When you complete something, your brain shifts from scanning to moving. It stops asking *what I should do* and starts *asking what's next*. That shift reduces anxiety.

Many people stay overwhelmed because they keep planning instead of finishing. Planning feels productive, but it does not close loops. Action does.

This doesn't mean you stop planning. It means you stop hiding in planning.

One win also builds trust: trust that you can follow through, trust that you can move forward even when things feel heavy, and trust that progress doesn't require perfection.

That trust is critical.

People who feel stuck often don't trust themselves, not because they're unreliable, but because urgency trained them to start fast and stop early. Incompletion became familiar.

One win interrupts that pattern.

It proves that you can finish.

This chapter is also about choosing the right win. The goal is not to overwhelm yourself with productivity. The goal is to create calm.

The right win reduces mental load.

Often, that means choosing a Bucket One task that has been weighing on you. Handle it. Close it. Remove it from your mental space.

Other times it means a small Bucket Two action that moves the future forward. Not everything. Just something.

Completion releases energy.

That energy fuels the next step.

This is why people feel better after cleaning one area, making one decision, or finishing one conversation. It's not about the task. It's about the signal it sends.

The signal is this: I am in control.

Control doesn't mean control over life. It means control over your response.

One win reminds you that you are not powerless. You are capable of movement.

This chapter also challenges the idea that progress must feel hard. Sometimes progress feels relieving. Sometimes it feels calming. Sometimes it feels simple.

Those moments matter.

You don't need to overhaul your life to feel better. You need to restore trust between your mind and your actions.

One win does that.

When things feel heavy, ask yourself a simple question: *What is one thing I can finish today?*

Not start. Finish.

Then do it.

Don't stack wins. Don't rush. Let the completion land.

That feeling is the beginning of momentum.

The power of one win is that it shifts your identity. You stop seeing yourself as overwhelmed and start seeing yourself as moving.

Movement changes perspective.

This gives you an immediate tool. Not tomorrow. Not after reading the book. *Right now.*

When life feels loud, when pressure builds, when clarity fades, return to one win.

It will restore calm faster than motivation ever could.

Lastly, you need to know how to maintain clarity when pressure increases and responsibility grows.

Chapter Twelve

CLARITY UNDER PRESSURE

How to stay grounded when life gets loud and responsibility increases.

Pressure doesn't mean something is wrong. Pressure means something matters.

Most people panic when pressure shows up. They assume it is a warning sign. A signal that they are failing or falling behind. So they rush. They react. They abandon structure in the very moments they need it most.

Clarity isn't the absence of pressure. Clarity is the ability to think accurately under pressure.

Life doesn't get quieter as you grow. Responsibility expands, expectations rise, opportunities increase, more people rely on you, and more decisions pass through your hands. Pressure isn't a phase. It's a companion.

The question is not how to avoid pressure. The question is how to remain grounded inside it.

The Three Buckets system was built for moments like these.

When life gets loud, the instinct is to abandon systems and rely on instinct. That is where most people get lost. Instinct under pressure is usually fear-driven. It shortcuts clarity. It pulls you back into urgency and misplacement.

The discipline is to return to structure.

Under pressure, you ask the same question you always ask: *What bucket does this belong in?*

Pressure tries to convince you that everything belongs in Bucket One. That lie creates panic. The buckets restore truth.

When pressure increases, Bucket One must become even more protected. You cannot afford to overload it. You must be ruthless about what truly requires immediate action.

When pressure increases, Bucket Two must remain steady. This is when people abandon long-term thinking and regret it later. Growth doesn't pause because things get hard. It becomes more important.

When pressure increases, Bucket Three gets louder. Thoughts multiply. Opinions increase. Doubt grows. Noise tries to take control. This is when boundaries matter most.

Clarity under pressure is not about doing more. It is about doing less with more intention.

Many people break under pressure because they try to hold everything at once. They stop trusting their system and start reacting to every input. That reaction creates exhaustion and mistakes.

The buckets prevent that.

This chapter is about trust: trust in the structure you've built, trust that you don't need to solve everything today, and trust that order will carry you through loud seasons.

Clarity under pressure also requires emotional regulation. Pressure triggers old patterns, survival instincts, the urge to overexplain, the urge to control, and the urge to fix everything immediately.

Awareness interrupts that urge.

You're allowed to pause even when things feel intense. Pausing doesn't mean neglect. It means choosing accuracy over reaction.

One of the most powerful skills you can develop is the ability to slow your response without slowing your progress.

Pressure doesn't demand speed. It demands precision.

Precision comes from clarity.

Clarity comes from placement.

When you feel pressure rising, return to basics: identify what must be handled now, schedule what matters, and release what is noise.

Then choose one win.

Pressure shrinks when progress is visible.

Another truth this chapter holds is that pressure often shows up right before alignment. Before growth. Before expansion. Before change. Many people misinterpret this moment and self-sabotage.

They pull back, doubt themselves, and abandon what they were building.

Clarity allows you to recognize pressure as a signal of movement, not danger.

You are not behind. You are in transition.

This is where leadership lives, not in calm moments, but in moments where things are uncertain and you still choose structure over chaos.

Living with clarity under pressure means you stop letting emotions make decisions for you. You acknowledge them without obeying them. You feel them without letting them drive.

You do not need to be fearless. You need to be organized.

This chapter closes the book by reinforcing the truth that clarity is a practice. Not a destination. You will return to the buckets again and again. Some days will be easier than others. Some seasons will test the system.

That is normal.

The power isn't in never feeling overwhelmed again. The power is in knowing exactly what to do when you do.

You now have a system to return to, a way to organize your mind, a way to protect your energy, and a way to move forward without panic.

Pressure will come. Let it.

You are no longer reacting to life. You are placing it.

This isn't a mindset. It's a system.

Use it daily. Let it grow with you. And move forward knowing you are no longer surviving the noise.

You are leading through it.

RETURNING TO THE BUCKETS

If this book did its job, you don't feel hyped right now.

You feel clear.

Not because life suddenly got easier, but because your mind finally has a place to put things.

That is the real win.

Most books try to leave you inspired. Inspiration fades. What lasts is orientation: knowing where you are, knowing what matters, and knowing what doesn't deserve your energy anymore.

The Three Buckets were never meant to change your life overnight. They were meant to change how you move through it every day.

You'll forget this system sometimes. You'll slip back into urgency, carry noise longer than you should, overload

Bucket One, neglect Bucket Two, and entertain Bucket Three more than you want to admit.

That does not mean the system failed.

It means you're human.

The difference now is awareness.

You'll notice sooner when your mind feels heavy, recognize when urgency is lying to you, and feel the moment stress shows up without a clear action attached to it. And when you do, you'll know what to do.

You will return to the buckets.

That return is the practice.

Clarity isn't something you achieve and keep forever. It's something you return to, again and again, especially when life gets loud.

There will be seasons where Bucket One demands more from you. Real emergencies. Real pressure. Real responsibility. In those seasons, the system protects you from panic. It keeps you from turning everything into a crisis. It keeps you focused on what truly needs attention.

There will be seasons where Bucket Two becomes the priority. Building. Healing. Growing. Creating. In those seasons, the system reminds you not to rush what takes time. It keeps you patient. Consistent. Grounded.

There will be seasons where Bucket Three feels over-whelming. Opinions multiply, comparisons creep in, and old doubts resurface. In those moments, the system gives you permission to release what doesn't require action.

The buckets move with you. They adapt. They stay simple.

That simplicity is the strength.

You don't need a complex framework to manage life. You need a reliable one, something you can access when you're tired, emotional, under pressure, or not feeling your best.

That is when systems matter most.

This book was never about doing more. It was about doing the right things at the right time with the right energy.

It was about reclaiming your mental space.

Mental space is where peace lives, where creativity lives, and where good decisions are made. When your mind is crowded, everything feels harder than it needs to be.

You were never meant to carry everything at once.

The buckets give you permission to stop trying.

As you move forward, keep this simple daily check-in by asking yourself one question in the morning and one question at night.

In the morning: *What bucket does today require my energy in?*

At night: What can I release before I sleep?

That alone will change how your days feel.

You'll also notice something subtle happening over time. Your relationships will improve. You'll respond instead of react, stop explaining yourself unnecessarily, and become more present.

Your confidence will grow. Not the loud kind, but the quiet kind that comes from knowing you can handle what matters and let go of what does not.

Your anxiety will lessen, not because life got perfect, but because your mind stopped treating everything like a threat.

You will trust yourself more.

Trust is the foundation of calm.

One of the most important things to remember as you leave this book is that clarity doesn't mean you stop caring. It means you care accurately. You give your energy where it matters and stop wasting it where it doesn't.

That is maturity.

That is leadership.

That is peace.

You are allowed to rest without guilt.

You are allowed to move slowly without falling behind.

You are allowed to say no without explaining.

You are allowed to prioritize yourself without apology.

None of that makes you careless. It makes you intentional.

The world will always try to rush you. It will always try to convince you that everything is urgent, that everyone's expectations matter, that your worth is tied to how much you carry.

You now know better.

You know that overwhelm is not a weakness.

You know that urgency is often a habit.

You know that stress comes from misplacement.

And you know how to correct it.

This system is yours now. Take it with you. Use it at work. In relationships. In leadership. In parenting. In building whatever you are building.

Let it evolve with you.

And when life feels heavy again, because it will, do not panic. Do not judge yourself. Do not spiral.

Return to the buckets. Handle what must be handled. Schedule what matters. Release what is noise.

Then choose one win.

That's how clarity is built. That's how peace is protected. That's how you stop reacting to life and start leading it.

Not once.

But daily.

And that is enough.

ABOUT THE AUTHOR

WALLO267 is proof that purpose has no borders. After serving twenty years behind bars, he turned his story into a global movement of resilience and reinvention. A *New York Times* bestselling author, cultural advisor at YouTube, former Chief Marketing Officer of Reform Alliance, and co-host of *Million Dollaz Worth of Game* (named by *The Hollywood Reporter* among the most powerful voices in podcasting, 2024), WALLO267 continues to merge impact and innovation. He uses partnerships, like his $4.5 million minority business initiative with Barstool Sports, his lifestyle brand ARPLNSNHOTLS, and his production company Nanny's House Entertainment, which develops and produces movies, TV series, books, and podcasts, to prove your past is data, not destiny.

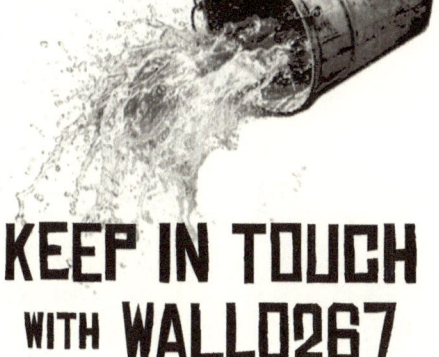

KEEP IN TOUCH
WITH WALLO267

Stay connected, stay inspired, and keep growing with me. I share daily messages, lessons, and moments to help you stay focused on becoming your best self.

Follow & connect on social:
Instagram • Facebook • TikTok • YouTube • X (Twitter)
@WALLO267

For speaking engagements, partnerships, and media inquiries:
✉ info@wallo267.co,
🌐 www.wallo267.co

Your journey matters.
Keep showing up for yourself every day.